Fr S
Ma

Who Farted?

Stories in verse for big & little kids

Who Farted?

Stories in verse for big & little kids

Written by Neil Crone

Illustrated by Wes Tyrell

ĕß

echo
BOOKS

An imprint of
Wintertickle PRESS

Copyright © 2012 Neil Crone
Illustrations copyright © 2012 Wes Tyrell

All rights reserved. No part of this information (publication or product) may be reproduced or transmitted in any form or by any means, electronic, mechanical, photocopying, recording, or otherwise, or stored in a retrieval system, without the prior written permission of Wintertickle Press.

Library and Archives Canada Cataloguing in Publication

Crone, Neil, 1960-
        Who farted?: stories in verse for big and little kids/Neil Crone;
Wes Tyrell, illustrator.

ISBN 978-1-894813-56-3

        1. Children's poetry, Canadian (English).
I. Tyrell, Wes, 1964- II. Title.

PS8605.R645W46 2012   jC811'.6   C2012-902539-9

Published by Echo Books, an imprint of Wintertickle Press
92 Caplan Avenue, Suite 155
Barrie, ON, Canada   L4N 0Z7
www.teacheasy.net

echo
BOOKS

Wintertickle PRESS

Printed and bound in Canada.

Cover: Wes Tyrell
Book Layout: Heather Down

For Duncan and Connor...the best teachers
a father ever had.

Table of Contents

Introduction

Almost from the moment my own two kids began to talk, I began writing poems. I love words and I love playing with words…and nobody is better at playing with words than little children who are just learning to talk. They talk all day long! They play with the new sounds they can make, they twist them this way and that, they fold them and toss them around and see what new forms they might take. All the while they are growing and learning to walk and falling down and getting up again and exploring their new world. Every day my kids gave me something new to write about. I just had to watch.

I hope you enjoy the stories in this book. I especially hope you may even see a little of yourself or someone you know in here. Most of these poems are based on or inspired by real people…or real animals. All wonderful personalities who have colored my life and made it more fun in one way or another. Life is beautiful and it's even better when it rhymes! Enjoy!

The Melderson's Dog is Sitting on Me

The Melderson's dog is sitting on me.
He's enormously heavy and hairy.
He's a sizeable pup and he won't let me up
and he smells sort of unsanitary.

The problem began at the start of the night
as the sun settled down in the west.
He tackled me hard as I cut through his yard
and proceeded to sit on my chest.

He's been on me now for an hour and a half
and he sure doesn't feel any thinner.
This mutt isn't fooling, he just started drooling
like maybe he wants me for dinner.

I'm flat on my back and my leg's gone to sleep
and I'm starting to feel kinda woozy.
But Rover's just sitting, with no signs of quitting
and believe me this dog is a doozy.

Yes, the Melderson's dog is sitting on me
and he's panting and stinky and fat.
If there's a dog on your street…when you go trick or treat
don't ever dress up like a cat.

OverDue

Overdue, yes overdue
these books are overdue.
They've been sitting on my dresser here
since 1942.

I know I'm s'posed to take them back
that's how the librairies do it.
And I always really meant to,
I just never got 'round to it.

Seems whenever I endeavour
to return them, I'm distracted.
Like one time I almost got there
then my wisdom teeth impacted.

Or once I got so close
there seemed no shadow of a doubt
that I'd return them there and then for sure...
then World War II broke out.

Another time I walked away
trying not to panic
as I heard, outside the library door,
the news of the Titanic.

There were countless other episodes
too many to relate
that always seemed to stop me
right outside the library gate.

And every one was horrible
and every one was sad.
Seems whenever I picked up those books
stuff happened that was bad.

So finally I decided
not to touch those books again.
And we've been free of catastrophe
since I can't remember when.

These books are overdue, it's true
but now, you see, they're mine.
To keep the world from further harm…I gladly paid the fine.

Hiram The Private Pirate

There are tall tales told on the seven salty seas
but the tallest that ever was told
is a whale of a tale 'bout a ship who set sail
with a captain who wasn't that bold.

Her name was the Gloria Doria Sneets
and the skipper was Hiram McFrimp.
As pirate ships go she was queen of the show,
but as pirates go he was a wimp.

Oh he wore all the stuff that a pirate should wear
and he knew all the good pirate words.
But his "Arrgh" lacked conviction, his "Yo!" was pure fiction
and his "Blow me down!" was for the birds.

See a pirate ship captain needs bluster and bluff
and a steely cold glint in his eye.
Hiram hated to fight, he was too darn polite
and in fact he was painfully shy.

His bloodthirsty crew would cry "Hullaballoo"
as they pulled alongside some poor ship.
Then Hiram would peak from his cabin and speak
"Hi there folks! Have you had a nice trip?"

Then there was the chap with an old treasure map
who said "X marks the spot where there's gold!"
The crew raced ashore to find treasure galore
but not Hiram, he thought he'd catch cold.

And one day they found a boat who'd struck ground
she was loaded with Spanish Dubloons.
Right by it they went, without taking a cent
'cause Hiram was watching cartoons.

And one stormy night, they were caught in a fight
and they loaded each cannon below.
But out stepped ol' Hiram, before they could fire 'em
and said, "Guys, I think we should go."

So one by one, as they missed out on fun
the crew of the Sneets started grumbling.
The word spread like heck, from the poop to the deck
and it sounded like mutiny mumbling.

Then just like you'd think, when the night was like ink
Old Hiram was jumped by surprise.
When they came to get him, poor Hiram just let 'um
'cause he'd just put his drops in his eyes.

Then they let down a boat, and they set him afloat,
with his books and his floss and canteen.
Then sailed into the west, to do what pirates do best,
that is steal stuff and swear and be mean.

Old Hiram just sobbed, on his sleeve as he bobbed
up and down on the waves of the ocean.
His heart was all hurt and his best pirate shirt
had been torn in that nasty commotion.

But after a while his face grew a smile
as a thought floated into his head.
Now he was free to be who he should be
he could lose the old life that he'd led.

And so with a book and a satisfied look
it is said that he drifted away.
"Why be a pirate when you just don't desire it?"
I think is what Hiram would say.

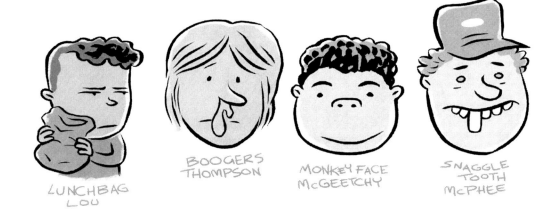

LUNCHBAG LOU

BOOGERS THOMPSON

MONKEY FACE McGEETCHY

SNAGGLE TOOTH McPHEE

Nick Name

Seems like every other kid I know
has got some name that's neat
like Jimmy Johnson's "Junkyard" and Stu Melman's "Stinky feet"
and Paula Parkill's "Putty Nose" and Willa Walsh is "Welch".
and everybody knows that Mitchell Keenan's name is "Beltch"
There's "Monkey Face McGeetchy" and there's
"Boogers Thompson" too
"Barf Bag Reynolds", what a guy,
and don't forget "P.U."
"Pencil's Martin", "Toots O'Shea", "Snaggle-tooth McPhee"
everybody's got a name that's cool
excepting me.
Sandy Sloan is called "The Bone"
her brother's name is "Wedgy"
and if you wanna see "The Zit"
just ask for Joe Pileggi.
"Recess" Horner, "Lunch Bag" Lou, and "Gotchies Mandalay"
I'd really love to have a name
that's that much fun to say.
I've tried out different handles, sure
but nothing seems to stick.
Maybe the real problem is
my name's already Nick!

Lasagna on Ya

Did you ever get Lasagna on ya,
sittin' there at dinner?
Or mustard from your hot dog on your white shirt;
that's a winner.

Or have you had a chunk of chocolate cheesecake
on your chin?
Then felt it slap into your lap
as company came in?

Or maybe you had messy mango muffin
in your gob.
Then opened up to say hello
and said you were a slob.

Or grabbed a greasy gravy boat
thinking you'd refill it.
Except you found that it was full
and then of course you spill it?

Or maybe messed with meat so tough
it was like cutting cable.
And when you really strained
that beef when flying 'cross the table!

Say, have you seen somebody else
squirt ketchup on their clothes
and then you laughed so hard
your milk came flying out your nose!

I've tried to eat all nice and neat
believe me it's no good
'cause everytime my food goes
everywhere but where it should.

Teeter-totter Toots

Don't ever try to Teeter-totter
with a guy named Toots.
He'll send you into outer space
and blast you from you boots.
He'll bounce that board against your butt
he'll really wreck your rear.
He'll send you soaring up so high
you'll fill with stratos-fear!
And what goes up comes down again
of course we all know that.
But did you know the higher up
the bigger is the splat?
I'm telling you, 'cause boy I know,
if you see Toots, just run.
The teeter up is thrilling
but the totter down's no fun.

Handsome Hank

Handsome Hank the tractor has unparalleled good looks.
He's the envy of each barnyard in the land.
His beauty has been boasted of in bulletins and books.
In the Farmer's Almanac they called him grand.

He's the picture of perfection from his bumper to his hitch.
Not a cylinder or valve is out of place.
No blossom in the world compares to Hank's hydraulic switch
and his fuel pump will cause your heart to race.

His tires are black as midnight, and his headlights blaze like stars
but the rest of Hank is candy apple red.
He gleams his grill at tourists taking pictures from their cars
parked to see this fetching fendered furrow-bred.

Gasping at his gorgeous gas tank, thrilling at his throttle
the crowd inside the pasture grows each day.
But Farmer Fletcher sadly sits and sips his soda bottle
and wishes these good folks would go away.

That tractor's handsome yessiree, the Farmer must confess.
Still he wishes things was like they was before
they used to plow and plant all day with nary time to rest.
Now he can't get Hank to do a single chore.

Hank hates the harrow, pooh-poohs the plough and simply won't endure
to taint his treads in stuff as plain as mud.
He will not entertain the thought of spreading horse manure.
In fact, as tractors go, Hank is a dud.

Now suddenly, amid the din of camera shutters clicking
Farmer Fletcher strolls down to Hank's side.
He walks around him slowly, gives his tires a little kicking
then leans in close to whisper an aside.

Hank's head-lamps suddenly flood wide, his diesel engine roars.
Farmer Fletcher jumps aboard and gives a wink.
And through the scattered crowd into the cornfield he now soars,
plowing sixteen hundred acres in a blink!

Hank plows and pulls and seeds and mows all day and into night
when finally he limps back to his bed.
The few onlookers still onlooking gasp upon the sight
of the dirty tractor, once so shiny red.

But in the dark cool of the barn, bathed by the setting sun
his radiator whispering fatigue,
Hank realizes that a life of fame was kind of fun,
but a working tractor's in another league.

He hears his fans disgruntled sighs and the slamming of car doors
and he knows inside that they will not return.
But a truly happy tractor is a tractor doin' chores,
a lesson even handsome tractors learn.

Farmer Fletcher rubs him down and greases every gasket
then lets Hank have a good long drink of fuel.
But there's a question on Hank's mind, and now he knows that he must ask it;
"Would you really have replaced me with a mule?"

Wipe out Warren

Here comes Wipe-out Warren
better give him lots of space.
You never know when he will go
careening 'round the place.

His balance is precarious
He's klutzy as they come.
The faintest breeze across his knees
can land him on his bum.

I guess the level in his head
is slightly out of whack,
one second he'll be even keel
then, 'boom', he's on his back!

It's so darn unpredictable
it just defies description.
One doctor has defined it as
"spontaneous conniption".

To ride like all the rest of us
is really what he'd like.
But you should see, he'll skin his knee
just thinking 'bout a bike.

He tried out for our baseball team.
That ended in disaster.
The ball was hit, he raised his mitt...
he shoulda raised it faster!

He joined us guys for hockey once
and gave us quite a scare.
We passed the puck, but just his luck,
it hit him 'you know where'!

I can't say why old Wipeout
carries 'round this klutzy curse.
I only know he's lucky
that his mother is a nurse.

Was there a Shark on Noah's Ark?

Was there a shark on Noah's Ark?
And if so, was he nice?
Or did some of Noah's passengers go missing
once or twice?
When they set out, the animals
came marching two by two.
But one by one, some disappeared.
Did Sharky eat a few?
He's innocent until his guilt
is proven, let's assume.
But still it's odd that Unicorn and Sharky
shared a room?

I Didn't Even Cry

Today I stepped outside
and got a snowball in the eye.
And even though it really stung,
I didn't even cry.

In school somebody accidentally
hit me with their rubber
and even though it hurt like stink
I didn't even blubber.

At lunch somebody scrunched my hand
inside a garbage pail
and even though I thought I'd die
I didn't even wail.

In gym I pranged my noggin'
on a hardwood balance beam
and even though the pain was fierce
I didn't even scream.

And coming in from recess
I got trampled in the hall
and even though I almost croaked
I didn't even bawl.

And then Stu Dickson's turtle bit me
during show-and-tell
and even though I near passed out
I didn't even yell.

Then later, walking home
I got a baseball in the beak
and even though I couldn't breathe
I didn't even shriek.

Each night I come home teary-eyed
my mother wonders why?
I tell her it's because all day
I didn't even cry!

All Dogs go to Heaven

If all dogs go to heaven
then I'm sure there's quite a crowd
and I wonder just who stoops and scoops
the dog poop off the clouds?

Haircut

Close the window,
shut the door
don't dare go outside.

Turn the lights out,
pull the drapes.
You gotta help me hide.

If my friends
come to the door,
just open it a crack,

and tell them that
I'm hiding out
until my hair grows back!

Baloney Butt

I have this friend, Baloney Butt
you might have seen him here.
He's kinda shy, I'll tell you why,
on account of the size of his rear.

His bum is big, oh yes indeed
in fact you could call it gigantic.
But his biggest part, is really his heart.
In spite of his rump, he's romantic.

He's got caring and kindness on every page;
yes, Baloney is really a lover.
But folks seldom look inside of the book.
They just cruelly cluck at the cover.

My big bottomed buddy's the best pal I have
and I hope that you'll give him a chance
'cause only a phony would look at Baloney
and see only the back of his pants.

I am Green from Halloween

I am green from Halloween,
in fact I'm feeling crummy.

Instead of in my loot bag
all my candy's in my tummy.

It started off so simply
just a candy kiss or two.

And then I saw a licorice pipe
I thought I'd like to chew.

Next I got a craving for some
caramel coated corn.

But I looked inside my loot bag
and I noticed it had torn.

And so to keep the rest of
all my swag from going south,

I proceeded to reroute my loot
directly to my mouth.

I haunted on undaunted
trick or treating door to door.

But from cramming all that candy in
my cheeks were getting sore.

I left the house that fateful night
dressed up just like a girl.

Now all I heard at every stop was
"Look, a darling squirrel!"

The night wore on and kids went home
and I thought it's time I followed.

But when I turned to go I tripped
and accidentally swallowed!

Imagine all that candy
squeezing slowly down my throat.

Now I know how Boa's feel
while gulping down a goat.

I've glanced into the science book
my aunt Cecilia bought us,

And I can tell you that it stretched me
from my epi to my glottis.

It crumpled up my larynx
and it left me at a loss.

To cry for help while it was making
Adam's apple sauce.

My tonsils took a trashing
as they stood their silent sentry.

Where would this gum ball glacier stop?
The answer's alimentary.

They could cancel Halloween today,
I wouldn't care a tuppence.

As I lie here and lament my loot
awaiting it's come-uppence.

The Thing In Gramma's Cellar

I think that there is something living in my Gramma's cellar.
But she just laughs and shakes her head each time I try to tell her.

I can't believe she hasn't heard the creaking every night
or the rumbling roar beneath the floor that makes my throat go tight.

Or the scratching on the floorboards like its coming through the wood!
Maybe 'cause she's older, Gramma doesn't hear so good?

I've warned her not to go down there, but Gramma never heeds it.
She takes down jars of beets and beans, you don't suppose she feeds it?

You don't suppose the creature's mind is mesmerizing Gramma's?
That thought's enough to make a fella pee in his pajamas.

It's clear that something must be done, and it's clear it's up to me.
Tonight I'm going down those stairs to see what I can see.

It's probably a monster or a mummy or a ghoul
or some dragon with huge yellow teeth, dripping dragon drool.

The more I think about this task the more I'm filled with dread.
On second thought, I think I'll send my sister down instead!

Dr. Prentice, the Mouse's Dentist

Dr. Prentice, the Mouse's Dentist
oh, but you should meet him!
He rushes to the Mouse's mouths
whenever they should need him.

Doesn't matter where he is,
or what the Doctor's doing,
he'll drop it for a mousey
who is having trouble chewing.

Once he walked a hundred miles
through snow drifts to his knees
all to help a tiny friend
floss out a chunk o' cheese.

And then there was the rat
who had a badly bent incisor.
He took out all his wisdom teeth
and left him none the wiser.

And in their holes, on quiet nights
you'll still hear mouses speak
of how he crowned a chap caught in a trap
then left without a squeak.

He's really quite mysterious
the way he'll come and go.
By George if you should ask me why?
Bi-cuspid, I don't know!

Why does he love the mice so much?
Why not a cow or sturgeon?
What drove him to become the world's
first Rodental Surgeon?

Perhaps his heart takes pity
on the mice because they're small?
Or maybe 'cause the Doc himself
is only two feet tall!

Sir Screamalot

Sir Screamalot, Sir Screamalot
likes to eat ice cream a lot.
He'll bellow on high beam a lot
until he gets his way.

Sir Screamalot, Sir Screamalot
methinks he does blaspheme a lot.
My mom's been refereem a lot
ever since he came to stay.

Sir Screamalot, Sir Screamalot
loves to blow off steam a lot.
My life's been one bad dream a lot
most each and every day.

Sir Screamalot, Sir Screamalot
shrieks like a chimpanzeemalot
and gets away scotfreemalot
no matter what I say!

Sir Screamalot, Sir Screamalot
why does it always seemalot
you always bother meemalot
each time you want to play?

There's Something in the Sandbox

There's something in the sandbox
I'm sure there's gotta be.
There used to be four of us here
and now there's only three.

There's something in the sandbox
I saw it move. Did you?
The three of us were playing,
now there's only me and you.

There's something in the sandbox
I think we better run.
Hey! What the heck is going on?
Now I'm the only one.

There's something in the sandbox
but it won't be coming back.
It goes away for hours
once it's had it's morning snack!

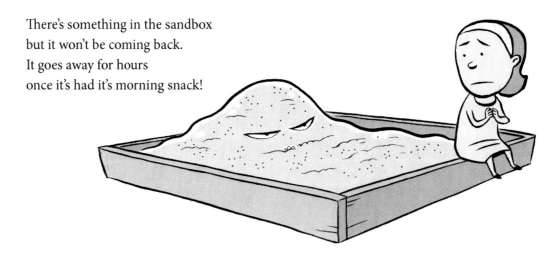

Library Card

I'm laying low.
I'm hiding out.
I'm taking furtive glances.
Watching every step I take
and taking fewer chances.
The FBI, the CIA,
and probably Scotland Yard
are on the lookout for the kid
who lost his library card!

Jack O'Lantern

My name is Jack O'Lantern
and you've probl'y seen my face.
I show it every Halloween
to brighten up the place.

I'm not much of a talker
but I've got a wicked smile.
And if you've got a moment
won't you stop and stare awhile.

Just look into my dancing eyes
and tell me what you see.
Witches, wolves and warlocks?
Yes, they're all inside of me.

Ghosts and Goblins? Got those too!
More spooks than I can handle.
But I promise they won't get you
if you don't blow out my candle!

Can We Get Some?

Can we get some?
Can we get some?
Boy do those look good!
No! They're not nutritious!
Why, they're barely even food.

Can we get some?
Can we get some?
There's a toy inside!
No! There's too much sugar!
And besides that it's deep-fried.

Can we get some?
Can we get some?
Can't we please just try it?
No! That stuff's not coming home!
Your father's on a diet.

Can we get some?
Can we get some?
Buy two and get one free!
No! You must be kidding!
That junk's full of MSG.

Can we get some?
Can we get some?
Mom! Your favourite flavour!
Well, okay, I guess this once,
I'll do *you* kids a favour.

Charlie

Hello God, are you listening?
It's me, my name is Kevin.
I wondered if you met my dog,
today he went to heaven.

Charlie is his name, God
and his hair is long and black.
And he really really loves it
when you scratch him on his back.

And could you tell the angels, God
to throw him lots of sticks.
And to give him cut up wieners
when they want him to do tricks.

And it's a good idea, God
to get some rawhide chews.
And if you don't , please don't get sore
when Charlie chews your shoes.

Be sure to let him out, God,
for a pee after he's fed.
And I'm sure you'll sleep much better God
with Charlie in your bed.

I hope one day that I will play
with him up in the stars.
Until then God, could you please keep
my dog away from cars?

The Bumber

Have you ever noticed when you wake up in bed
that the hair is all mussed on the top of your head?
And the covers you pulled up have now been pulled down
and you look for who did it, but there's no one around?

Has your pillow been scrunched, and it used to be neat?
And the sheets are all chilly down there by your feet?
And your tongue feels as though you've been chewing on flies?
Not to mention the gunk that's been globbed in your eyes.

Who is it, you ask, who has drooled on your hand?
And your foot is asleep and you don't understand?
I'll tell you who does this, he's known as the Bumber,
a creature who only comes out when we slumber.

Where the Bumber comes from, well, no one really knows.
He's gone when we wake, we don't see where he goes.
But one thing's for sure, as we slip into sleep,
into our bedrooms the Bumber will creep.

But the Bumber's not bad, let me please calm your fears
without him you might sleep for hundreds of years.
For the work that he does and the length that he goes to
is to see that you get out of bed when you're s'pose to.

How was it you asked, that you finally awoke,
on that morning you found your alarm clock was broke?
Who opened your eyes on that horrible morning
the school bus came early and gave you no warning?

The Bumber, I'll bet, was who got you to school
with his icy cold breathe and his hideous drool.
His long warty fingers, gently twisting your hair
made sure that when breakfast arrived, you'd be there.

And who scrunched your pillow so gently? It seems,
that the Bumber was coaxing you in from your dreams.
And what of the gunk in your eyes? Well I think,
that the Bumber arrived at your thirty-ninth wink.

So don't scorn the Bumber, please thank him instead
for staying up late to get you out of bed.
You may sleep in forever, if he ever gets fed up.
Give the Bumber a break, and for Pete's sake get up!

I Just Squashed a Bug

I just squashed a bug
and now I'm having second thoughts.
What if he was the very last bug
who had those greenish dots?

What if he was a doctor bug
who discovered bug penicillin?
I don't think I'd have squished so hard
if I'd known it was him I was killin'.

Maybe he was a statesman bug
with a plan for World bug peace?
Rushing to the Bug U.N.
with an urgent bug Press Release?

The more I think about it all,
the guiltier I feel.
To know that 'cause of me
there's an empty chair at some bug meal.

God, if you are listening,
I'm sorry I was such a schlep.
And also God, while I'm walking home,
could you please watch your step?

Bob the Basement Blob

I am Bob, the basement blob.
I live down in the dark.
I lurk in cobwebbed corners
like some sort of shadow shark.

I wait there in the blackness
in the creaky cranky gloom,
awaiting some stray ankle
I can grab and drag to doom.

I know you know I'm down here
I have heard your startled steps.
I've watched each time you creak the door
and peer down in the depths.

I also know you're curious.
You're dying to find out
what all that burbling, bubbling,
babbling, noise is all about.

So come on down, I promise
everything will be all right.
As long as you will promise that
you won't turn on the light!

Climbing Mike

I am Mike
and what I like
is climbing most of all.
It doesn't matter what it is
as long as it is tall.

I climb on chairs
I climb on stairs
I climb up on the bed.
I climb until there's nothing left
that is, above my head.

I have no fear
and it is clear
in fact it is my feeling.
There's nothing that could stop me now
except maybe...the ceiling?

Jaloppy-pops

Say have you tried Jaloppy-pops?
They're fun! They're cool! They're wild!
They're frozen autos on a stick,
but they're old fashioned styled.

This Model T is marvelous!
Hey, try this tasty Tucker.
This Edsel's oh so edible.
A six cyllindered sucker!

A carmel covered Corvair Cream!
A treat at any speed.
How 'bout that Rhubard Rambler?
Wow! A Nash is what I need.

A lemonade LaSalle is nice,
the Ford is fairly fizzy.
Say, which one really turns your crank?
The tangerine Tin Lizzy?

Yes, pick up some Jaloppy-pops
but make sure the pack is dusty,
like all unique antiques, they taste much better
when they're rusty!

Who Farted?

Who farted? Who farted?
Say who cut the cheese?
Who started the stink that is blowin' in the breeze?
Who shooted the toot that brought me to my knees?
Can't somebody tell me, oh please!

Who farted? Who farted?
Man, who dropped a rose?
Who made the nasty that's now in my nose?
Who owns the backside from whence this arose?
It follows wherever I goes!

Who farted? Who farted?
Whoa! Who sliced the brie?
Who launched the butt missile marked S.B.D.?
Whoever did that, farts professionally!
Hey maybe it could've been me?

Up the Wall

I'm gathering pillows and blankets and stuff
'cause I'm driving my Mom up the walls.
And I'm piling them up in a big fluffy heap
so she won't hurt herself if she falls.

What if...

What if for hands, you had pots and pans
or for feet you had pieces of rope?

And what if your middle was shaped like a fiddle
or your butt was a big bar of soap?

Would it seem very weird if your knees had a beard?
Or your elbows were made out of cake?

And what if instead, on the front of your head,
there wasn't a nose, but a rake?

Would you think it's a scream, or some kind of bad dream
if you woke up with bottle-cap eyes?

And what if for toes you had hooks to hang clothes?
Now wouldn't that be a surprise?

Could you say 'What the heck', if in place of your neck,
an accordion flopped all around?

Would you think it a joke, every time that you spoke,
all you heard was accordion sound?

'What if?' and 'Could you?' and 'How 'bout?' is fun too.
These are all games that I love to play.

An imagination's the best vaccination
to ward off the boringest day.

Toboggan Noggin'

Folks call me Toboggan Noggin'
every time they see me.
Sometimes they wanna shake my hand
sometimes they wanna ski me.

You see my head is flat and that
is perfect for downhilling
and so I charge a buck a ride
and man I've made a killing.

They wax me up with shampoo
then they flip me upside down.
Then they schuss down through the slopes
for ropes they use my double crown.

They laugh and shout and scream a lot
as though the trip were scary.
One girl rode down and said
the ride was positively 'hairy'.

You probably think a bean like this
would be a real pain.
But there's no doubt the friends I've made
are worth the odd migraine.

There's really only one thing
I don't like about this head.
Each night my big Toboggan Noggin'
slides right out of bed!

Sullen McMullen

If you're down in the dumps, with a case of the grumps
and you're feeling as blue as they come.
And you've had it with noise about sharing your toys,
and you've gargled a gallon of glum.

If you're looking for treats but only find beets
and you got a new bike but it's snowing.
Then listen to me, my advice is for free
there's a fellow who's really worth knowing.

McMullen's his name and sullen's his game,
he's the miserable master of mopes.
When it comes to pathetic this guy is athletic,
he's smashing at dashing of hopes.

A kill-joy, a keener, a real make-a-scener
he's worrisome, wretched and wistful.
The guy's always crying. It's true, I'm not lying
he uses tissues by the fistful.

He's soaking in sorrow, lives in fear of tomorrow
give him any sport and he'll spoil it.
And the pleasure he takes, for criminy sakes
at flushing his dreams down the toilet!

Now how could it be, beneficial to me
to get to know him you may query.
Yes I know that he's sad, but that's not all that bad,
if you listen I'll tell you my theory.

For sure he's a frowner, a definite downer,
as warm as a wet woolen sweater.
But if you're feeling sullen, one day with McMullen
is bound to make you feel much better!

Eudora Zanns

Eudora Zanns collected cans,
collected cans aplenty.
She liked the ones that looked brand new
not those that were all denty.

Eudora Zanns adored her cans
and stacked them every morning.
Until one day to her dismay,
they wobbled without warning.

Eudora Zanns had made no plans
for toppling tins you see
and so she froze, the story goes,
at this cantastrophe.

Eudora Zanns with folded hands
watched as her containers
did soda slips and cream corn kips
and frozen grape juice gainers.

Eudora Zanns now understands
it makes much better sense
to toss the few that look brand new
and keep the ones with dents.

New Shoes Nelson

New Shoes Nelson runs along
at sixty miles an hour.
Filled with super rubberific
hi-test sneaker power.

He's faster than a turbo train
or supersonic jet.
He says he's got the fastest shoes
a guy could ever get.

We just laugh and you should know
the reason why we scoff
is New Shoes Nelson can't slow down
to get the darn things off.

Ian Resnick

Ian Resnick's famous
and his glory grows and grows.
And it's all because there's nothing
Ian won't put up his nose.

It started with a frozen pea
he sucked it up like that!
Then he snorted in a marble
and Stu Blakely's baseball hat.

Pencils, pens and paper planes,
he sniffed them up his snoot.
Sammy Simpson's soccer ball?
He snuffled in to boot!

A cadillac, a coke machine
a walrus? Wait...a whale!
There really isn't anything
that Ian won't inhale!

All that junk goes up his nose
and God knows where he stows it.
I just don't wanna be around
when Ian Resnick blows it!

Leave those leaves!

Leave those leaves, leave those leaves
oh leave those leaves alone.
Inside that moldy, mildewed mess
live creatures still unknown.

Leave those leaves, leave those leaves
don't think of jumping in.
Your chance of jumping out again
is really very thin.

Leave those leaves, leave those leaves
if you have to, cross the street.
You're not a kid to what's inside,
you're something nice to eat.

Leave those leaves, leave those leaves
Warning! Danger! Yikes!
Two guys rode through that pile at lunch
now all that's left are bikes.

Leave those leaves, leave those leaves
what's in there is the worst.
If you go in, you won't come out
and you wouldn't be the first.

Measles

Today we all go to the gym
to get our shots for measles.
I wouldn't say I'm scared
I'm just a little ill at easels.

I'd gladly be the first in line
but heavens, golly-geesles.
I'd rather stay here in the class
and learn my ABC'sles.

And please don't misconstrue
the noisy knocking of my kneesles.
That's only just because I'm feeling like
I have to peesles.

And if my teeth are chattering,
I'm just chilly from the breezels
and that water in my eyes
is just because I have to sneezles.

But really, though I'm acting brave
and strong like some big cheesels.
The truth is that I wish these shots
could wait until grade threezels.

Peanut Butter and Honey Bees

Peanut Butter and Honey Bees are buzzing 'round my roses
they've got chunky chunks of peanut gunk stuck on their cheeks and noses.

Their wings are soft and sticky which makes aviation trying
you will know of what I speak if you've tried peanut butter flying.

Yet still they zip stoutheartedly 'round garden, shrubs and lawn,
the workers ever working as the drones drone on and on.

Like other bees their honey comes from pollen in the flowers,
But gathering the peanut butter, that can take them hours.

Their eyes are ever open as they buzz along in bunches,
seeking solitary sandwiches or lost leftover lunches.

They'll even swipe it from the jar, it's amazing how they do it,
two hundred bees hold down the lid, while a hundred more unscrew it!

A word of warning to all kids who reach the table late,
if these swarming swindlers get there first, they may just take your plate.

But if you wish to see the most fantastic thing alive,
then follow as they fly back to their sweet peanutty hive.

There deep within the sweetness of the golden dripping halls,
and the pleasant pungent perfume of the peanut butter walls,

The Queen, in regal gooeyness, sits proudly on her throne,
preening her antennae with expensive honeycomb.

She looks concerned and worried, though I know this sounds incredible.
Wouldn't you be worried too, if your house were so spreadable?

Narrative Ned

Narrative Ned loved a story at bed
a comedy, romance or drama.
And he cared not a darn who was telling the yarn
whether Mommy or Daddy or Gramma.

Ned enjoyed fishin', and liked television
but what he loved most completely and totally,
was getting in bed, putting pillow to head
and ending each day anecdotally.

Each night, were he able, he would feast on a fable
from Aesop or Potter or Grimm.
Without predilection he gobbled up fiction
from *The Wizard of Oz* to *Lord Jim*.

He drank pails and pails of old wives tales
in languages from all round the world.
He sucked up each saga, and in fact he went gaga
when the dead sea scrolls were unfurled.

The problem arose when he ran out of prose
he'd read every book in the land.
He's a pitiful sight as he wanders each night,
with his library card in his hand.

With no words left for Ned, he just sits there in bed
and believe me he's tried counting sheep.
Ned's in dire need of a good book to read
and until then he can't go to sleep.

Drive-In

We're going to a Drive-in
yeah, we're gonna have some fun.
On the playground in our PJs
as we watch the setting sun.

Then we'll all attack the snack bar
snarfing candy, coke and chips.
We'll be pounding back the popcorn
'til we cannot feel our lips.

Then we'll start a back seat pillow fight
a real wide open brawl.
Then the fight will end abruptly
when my brother starts to bawl.

Then we'll jostle and we'll jockey
and we'll all scream "I can't see!"
And then right at all the good parts
one by one we'll have to pee.

Then we'll ask our folks what's goin' on,
in the car that's right beside.
Then we'll open up a window
and we'll let the bugs inside.

Then before the second feature
we'll go back for onion rings.
Then we'll all spend thirty minutes
getting Billy off the swings.

Then we'll just get settled nicely
like a cozy little bunch.
Then right at the movie's climax
one of us will lose his lunch.

Then Mom will start to say stuff
that we're not supposed to hear.
Then Dad will say it louder
as he puts the car in gear.

Then home we'll drive and soon
we'll all have closed our sleepy eyes.
Then Mom and Dad will smile and say
we love you little guys.